56

My Book and Heart
Shall never part

WITCH'S BREW

GOOD SPELLS

for

LOVE

WISDOM

from

WITCH BREE

CHRONICLE BOOKS

DEDICATION: *For my best friend and heart sister,*
Abra Ohlinger, a Goddess of Love in her own right.

© 2001 Herter Studio · Design and Illustration by Margo Chase

Edited by Julie Winokur

All rights reserved. Printed in Hong Kong.

10 9 8 7 6 5 4 3 2 1

ISBN 0-8118-2847-6

Distributed in Canada by Raincoast Books

9050 Shaughnessy Street

Vancouver, B.C. V6P 6E5

Chronicle Books LLC

85 Second Street

San Francisco, CA 94105

www.chroniclebooks.com

Witch's Brew was conceived and produced by Herter Studio.

432 Elizabeth Street, San Francisco, CA 94114

books@herterstudio.com

WITCH'S BREW

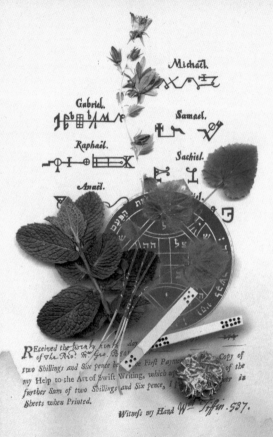

Michael.

Gabriel.

Samael.

Raphael.

Sachiel.

Anaël.

Received the twenty ninth day
of the Rñ. Mr. Geo. Bryan ... Copy of
two Shillings and Six pence be the First Payment ... of the
my Help to the Art of Swift Writing, which up ... er in
further Sum of two Shillings and Six pence, I ...
Sheets when Printed.

Witness my Hand Wm Tiffin. 537.

Spells for....

We live in all things;

All things live in us.

We dedicate this

Practice to others,

To celebrate the joy of living.

—ANCIENT
INCANTATION

R Eceived ...
of The Rev.d Mr Geo. Beau...
two Shillings and Six pence being th... ... of the
my Help to the Art of Swift Writing ... ... of the
further Sum of two Shillings and Six pence, I promi... ... er in
Sheets when Printed.

Witness my Hand W.m ...ffin .537.

Introduction

S O M E people
are just born W I T C H E S.
OTHERS DABBLE IN THE CRAFT BEFORE
THEY BECOME AWARE OF THEIR INNATE POWER.
For me, magic made its presence known very
early. Before I learned to read, I already knew
my astrological sign; by the time I was five, I
had learned the medicinal uses of herbs from
my Aunt Edith. She was my mentor, and
though she would have sooner called herself a
medicine woman than a witch, she was wise
in the ways of magic.

I

LIKE many others
BEFORE ME, LOVE SPELLS marked
my entry into the PRACTICE. At 13, I
cast my first love spell. Instantly, my best
friend became the object of AMOROUS
attention from a previously disinterested
suitor. Since then, I have had many years
and ample opportunity to perfect this
most joyous aspect of the CRAFT.
I have watched these spells kindle
and keep love's passion alive
time and time again.

ANY metaphysician
WILL TELL YOU that the most common
requests for help involve matters of the
HEART. Witchcraft is based on the
knowledge that our destinies lie in our own
hands, even where LOVE is concerned. So
why SUFFER the slings and arrows of love
gone wrong when you can DO SOMETHING
about it? Why spend a Saturday evening
alone when you already know the object of
your desire? And why doubt your
own power to attract love when a little
herbal chemistry can make you
virtually IRRESISTIBLE?

MAGIC NOT ONLY INFLUENCES
desired outcomes, but EMPOWERS
one's self and fosters personal growth. What
better way to begin this process than with spells
for love: spells that create the potential for
love, draw the attention and devotion of a
lover, strengthen the union between an
existing couple, invoke sexual magic, heal a
broken heart, and perhaps most importantly,
fill your own heart with love and compassion
for yourself. Inside this book are secret recipes
for aphrodisiacs, ritual celebrations for the
high holidays of L O V E, and insight
into the mysterious realm of the
MOON and the stars.

FOR MAXIMUM POWER,
LOVE SPELLS require you to use HERBS and
ASTROLOGICAL SIGNS with specific properties that
correspond to your desired outcome. If you want to
strike up a conversation with the HANDSOME, shy
fellow at work, try it when the MOON is in Gemini,
the best time for communication. If, after a few
successful dates, you are looking for things to
heat up, fix an **aphrodisiac** dinner one
Scorpio moon evening, the most sensual of
times. If you want to rekindle a long-lost love,
try a Cancer moon, when sentiments run high.
As ever, timing is **everything**,
and certain days are made
for LOVE.

THE **MAGIC** GUIDING THE SPELLS
in this book is white, used only to bring light
and love into people's lives. But beware the
power of these spells! Avoid some of my early
mistakes, like when I tried to help a girlfriend
and ended up being pursued instead. I not only
attracted undesired advances, I *LOST* a friend
in the process. The power you are wielding is
no small thing, and the more you practice, the
more **potent** your magic will be.

BECOMING a good **witch**
IS EASY. With DESIRE, a loving attitude,
a few natural **ingredients,** and a dash of
MAGIC, these custom-crafted recipes will
cook up exciting **flirtations,** enchanted
courtships, and *LASTING LOVE.* My hope
is that you and your loved ones will reap the
benefits of this timeless wisdom. Then,
in accordance with the grand tradition,
PASS IT ON.

Practical Magic

ANY **GOOD WITCH** KNOWS
that the BEST ingredients can be found in
your kitchen or your own back yard. Many
plants now thought of as weeds have great
healing powers and MAGICAL properties.
Most of the herbs and essential oils in this book
have become quite commonplace. With the
plethora of **aromatherapy** products now
available, most oil essences and scented candles
can be bought commercially. For the more
unusual ingredients, try your local health
food market, herbalist, or
metaphysical store.

Rose

OTHERWISE, try the
WITCH'S PANTRY at the back of
the book for alternative resources.
While all these ingredients are harmless,
consult your PHYSICIAN if you have any
sensitivities or allergies.

Phases of the Moon

PERFORMING A SPELL at the OPTIMAL TIME
in the LUNAR CYCLE will **maximize your power**.
As you read the spells in this book, keep this
elemental **m a g i c** in mind:

EACH LUNAR CYCLE begins with a "NEW" phase
when the moon lies between the sun and the earth so
the illuminated side cannot be seen from earth. The
moon gradually "WAXES" until it has moved to the
opposite side of the earth. When the moon has
reached the far side of the earth, its lit side faces
us in the "FULL" moon phase. It then begins
to "WANE" until it reaches the New
Moon phase again.

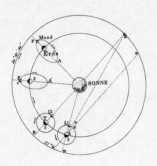

THE ENTIRE CYCLE takes a MONTH,
during which the moon orbits the earth. To
determine the **sun sign** governing the moon, you
will need a celestial guide or almanac. My favorite is
Llewellyn's DAILY PLANETARY GUIDE.
The moon moves from sign to sign every
two to three days.

The
SPELLS

FIRST PENTACLE OF VENUS:
BRINGS FRIENDSHIP TO THE POSSESSOR.

Enticing New Love

LOVE ALTAR

AN *ALTAR* IS A PLACE OF P O W E R
— your personal power — where you can make
MAGIC. It should be an expression of your
deepest self, FILLED WITH ARTIFACTS that hold
personal **resonance**. Allow your altar to
be a work-in-progress that **c h a n g e s**
with the seasons and reflects
your inner cycles.

To CREATE YOUR ALTAR, find
a small table and drape it in richly colored,
luxurious fabrics — perhaps red satin or a
burgundy velvet scarf. Take one red and one
pink candle, and arrange them around a sweet-
smelling incense such as amber, rose, or
jasmine. Decorate your altar with tokens that
represent love to you: a heart-shaped chunk of
ruby glass, potpourri made with ROSE and
AMETHYST, a PHOTO OF YOUR LOVER. Fridays are
the time for spelling love, right before DAWN.
Before you light your candles, anoint
them with a love oil you select from
the following pages.

SCENT YOUR WRISTS, your throat, and your left breast over your HEART with the same oil. Jasmine and rose have very powerful LOVE VIBRATIONS to attract and charm a lover. If you desire sexual results, look into the flame of the red candle; if your desire is affection or flirtation, look at the pink candle instead. This simple spell, said aloud, will create loving magic:

> *Venus, cast your light on me,*
> *A Goddess for today I'll be.*
> *A lover, strong and brave and true,*
> *I seek as a reflection of you.*

LOVER'S MOON

TO ATTRACT *new* LOVE, TWO
DAYS before the FULL MOON, take a pink votive
candle and place it inside your cauldron or any
large metal pot. Lay a rose and a bell beside the
cauldron and your altar. Use either rose or
apple-blossom essential oil to anoint the
candle's wick. For the next two nights, cup
the candle in your hands and direct LOVING
THOUGHTS into its flame. On the night
of the FULL MOON, take a thorn
from the rose and **c a r v e** the
name of your heart's desire
into the candle's wax,
reciting:

I will find true love.

LIGHT THE PINK CANDLE
and ring the bell thrice, saying:

As this candle begins to burn, a lover true will I earn.
As this flame burns ever higher, I will feel my lover's fire.

RING THE BELL three more times
and watch the candle BURN completely.

Brew of Mandrake

ATTRACTING *that* ATTRACTIVE STRANGER

DON'T TELL ME you have **never** had a brief
but MEANINGFUL encounter at your local café
or exchanged long, **lustful** glances on
the bus crossing town.

SHYNESS TIED YOUR TONGUE, and now your
only HOPE is that chance will bring you together.
Try this surefire attraction spell:

TAKE A MAN-SHAPED MANDRAKE ROOT
(commonly available at herbalists and
metaphysical shops), or any statue,

photograph, or figure of a man.
Place it on your ALTAR and surround the
figure's base with red and pink rose petals, and red
and pink candles. Place **two** goblets of red wine
beside this arrangement and BURN candles every night
for a week starting on Friday, VENUS' DAY. Sip from
one of the goblets, and recite:

Merry stranger, friend of my heart,
Merry may we meet again.
Hail, fair fellow, friend well met,
I share this wine and toast you,
As we merry meet and merry part
And merry meet again.

MAKE SURE YOU LOOK YOUR BEST,
as you will *SOON* lock eyes again.

EARTH:

COMPARED SYMBOLICALLY TO THE WOMB, SHE OFTEN APPEARS

IN MYTHOLOGY AS A NURTURING, FEMALE DEITY.

OIL *of* LOVE

ON A MOONLIT NIGHT, **indulge** in this
SENSUALLY SATISFYING ritual bath that will make your
skin glow and will surround you with a seductive aura.

It also makes an ideal, sexy tub for two.

Into a HOT, STEAMY BATH add:

3 ounces apricot kernel oil

3 ounces sweet almond oil

1 ounce aloe vera gel

1/2 ounce rosewater

13 drops jasmine essential oil

6 drops rose essential oil

SHAKE THE MIXTURE TOGETHER
and pour as much as you like into your bath.
(The **ingredients** must be premixed so the
POWER of the oils isn't diluted by the water before
their MAGICAL PROPERTIES bond.)

AS YOU UNDRESS, imagine you are preparing for
your lover. Sprinkle dried **chamomile** flowers
and yarrow into the hot bath to steep. Light a rose
or red candle (FOR PASSION) and say:

My heart is open, my spirit soars.
Goddess bring my love to me. Blessed be.

AS YOU SOAK, **DREAM** of what you'll do
when the **opportunity** arises and bask in the
rosy glow of this bath brew.

ULTIMATE GLAMOUR

FEW PEOPLE KNOW that the **origin**
of the word GLAMOUR comes from the 17th-
century Scottish word "glamour," which means to
cast a spell or ENCHANTMENT over anyone who
LOOKS UPON YOU.

DURING THE WAXING MOON, take the **rings**,
necklace, and **earrings** you are planning to
wear during a special tryst and lay them on your
altar to imbue them with magic. Mix together the
dried herbs *vervain, thistle, chamomile,* and
elder flower. Cover your jewelry with
the herb mixture and then sprinkle
salt on top. Hold the jewelry in
your hands and chant:

Bless these jewels and the hand and heart
of the wearer with the light of heaven above.
May all who look upon me
see me through the eyes of love.

SPELLBINDING *with* HEARTSTRINGS

ON A SMALL PIECE OF PAPER, write the NAME of your would-be LOVE in red ink and roll up the scroll. ANOINT the paper with rose or amber essential oil. Tie the scroll with RED threads, incanting one line of the following spell per knot:

One to seek my love, one to find my love,
One to bring my love, one to bind my love,
Forever bound together as one,
So mote it be. This charm is done.

KEEP THE LOVE SCROLL under a candleholder with red candles at the north corner of your altar until your **will** is done. Make sure of your desire; THIS SPELL IS LASTING.

L___ the 21__ Day of *Oct*__

R Received of *the Master & Wardens of the Stationers Comp*
the Sum of *Fifty Five Pounds* 19ℓℓ 2ₛ
being in full for *Fifty Four Pound*
in the Capital and Principal Stock
of the Governor and Company of Merchants of Great-Britain,
Trading to the South-Seas, and other Parts of America, and for
Encouraging the Fishery, &c. this Day Transferred in the said
Company's Books, unto the said *the Master & Wardens*

Witness, By
R 819 *Jℓ Drew* *Lewis Vanden Enden*

LOVER'S TEA

HERE'S A QUICK RECIPE to
create **exactly** the right mood for a
ROMANTIC EVENING.

Stir together in a clockwise motion:

1 ounce dried hibiscus flowers
1 ounce dried and pulverized rosehips
1/2 ounce dried lemon balm
1/2 ounce dried mint (ideally peppermint)
1/2 ounce meadowsweet

Store this herbal concoction in a dark,
LIDDED JAR OR TIN. (It will keep for one year,
after which you can recycle the herbs as a
BLESSING *for the* HEARTH *fire*.)

WHEN YOU ARE READY to brew the tea,
pick your most **s a c r e d** teapot and pour boiling
water over the herbs, two teaspoons for each cup of
water. Say the following S P E L L aloud during
the five minutes it takes for the tea to steep,
and visualize your H E A R T ' S D E S I R E :

Herbal brew of love's emotion,
With my wish I fortify.
When two people share this potion
Their love shall intensify
As in the Olde Garden of Love.

SWEETEN TO TASTE with honey and SHARE this
luscious L I B A T I O N with the one you
L O V E .

31

LASTING
DEVOTION

To Win the Female: HOLD THIS SEAL PRESSED AGAINST THE
LIPS BEFORE GOING OUT, AND YOU MAY WIN THE LOVE AND
COMPLIANCE OF THE ENTIRE FEMALE SEX.

PILLOW TALK

TO SECURE LASTING LOVE from
a nascent romance, a LOVE PILLOW can cast a
powerful, binding spell. This spell works best if you
use a soft, homemade pillow.

ON A FRIDAY, take two yards *of* pink satin fabric
and stuff it with SOFTEST goose down and the dried
petals of a red rose you've grown or received from
your LOVER. Sew it with GOLDEN thread
while you whisper:

Here rests the head of my true mate fair.
Nightly rapture is ours to share. So mote it be.

ANOINT THE THREAD with amber and rose oil,
especially when you "ENTERTAIN."

DREAMING DESTINY

THIS CHARM WILL help you see whether
newfound interest will become LONG-TERM.
If you or your lover lack clarity on this issue, your
dreams can guide you. Arrange a romantic evening
and prepare this amulet for CLAIRVOYANCE.

TAKE A SMALL RED VELVET or satin pouch (a folded
scarf will also do), and stuff it with lavender, thyme,
cinnamon, cloves, a vanilla bean pod, and a drop
of jasmine oil. Tie the ends **together** and hold
the pouch in both hands until your warmth and
ENERGY fully infuse the potpourri. Recite:

Venus guide my dreams tonight – Is he the one?

34

TUCK YOUR AMULET INTO a pillowcase before bedtime. Upon waking, ask yourself or your beau about the night's dreams. You will receive your answer IMMEDIATELY.

VENUS: GODDESS OF LOVE

BINDING LOVE POTION

To ensure a faithful relationship, gather **magnolia buds** under the cover of NIGHT in a WAXING MOON. Sweeten with honey and brew in a tea, sprinkle in a salad, or stir into a soup.
Chant this simple SPELL as you stir:

Lover be faithful, lover be true.
This is all I am asking of you.
Give thy heart to nobody but me.
This is my will.
So mote it be.

BEFORE YOU AND YOUR LOVER SHARE this
special treat together, whisper this wish:

Honey magnolia, Goddess' herb,
Perform for me enchantment superb,
Let (name of lover) and I be as one.
As ever, harm to none.
With this, the spell is done.

THIS MUST BE SEALED with a KISS between
you and your LOVER. Then feed your lover,
whom you wish not to STRAY, and his
loyalty will **n e v e r** sway.

37

BELLES LETTRES
that BIND

LOVE LETTERS ARE *an*
ANCIENT ART that always **deepens intimacy**.
What **heart** doesn't SURGE when the object of
affection pours PASSION onto the printed
page? Magic ink, prepared paper, and
MAGIC wax will seal the deal.

TAKE A SPECIAL SHEET OF PAPER (sumptuous
handmade or creamy watermarked stationery is
ideal) and write with a MAGICAL colored ink —
red **dragon's blood** is available at most
metaphysical shops, or try the
"Enchantment Ink" spell that follows.

PERFUME THE LETTER with your signature scent or an oil your lover has appreciated, like amber, vanilla, or ylang-ylang. Seal it with a wax you have also scented with one precious drop of essential oil and, of course, a KISS.

BEFORE YOUR LOVE LETTER IS DELIVERED, light a candle anointed with your preferred scent and intone:

Eros, speed my message on your wings of desire.
Make my lover burn with desire.

MAKE SURE you send your letter RSVP.

ENCHANTMENT INK

IF YOU ARE **LUCKY** ENOUGH *to* LIVE
in the COUNTRY or near a wild and weedy meadow,
you can easily find **pokeberries**. Poisonous when
eaten, these magenta berries make wonderful homemade ink. You can imbue this wine-colored ink with
magical powers with this simple spell.

DURING THE WANING MOON, fill a vial with
dark red ink and add the juice from the crushed
pokeberries. Add a few drops of **burgundy** wine
from the bottom of your LOVER'S glass and
one drop of a fruited essential oil such
as apple blossom, apricot,
or peach.

ADVENTUROUS WITCHES sometimes prick
their fingers and add a droplet of BLOOD,
as well. Incant aloud:

By my hand, this spell I have wrought.
With this sacred ink, I will author my own destiny,
And have the happy love I sought.
Blessed be.

NOW WRITE THE FATE you envision
for yourself and your lover with
enchanted ink.

GYPSY LOVE HERBS

MANY A GYPSY WOMAN has **enjoyed** the fruits of **long-lasting** LOVE by reciting this charm while mixing rye and pimento into almost every dish. While stirring in these AMOROUS herbs, recite:

Rye of earth, pimento of fire,
Eaten surely fuels desire.
Serve to he whose love I crave
And his heart I will enslave!

GARDEN *of* EARTHLY DELIGHTS

A GREAT RELATIONSHIP can be **cultivated,** literally. BY PLANTING and carefully tending flowers that have **special** properties — like night-blooming jasmine for heightened SENSUALITY, or lilies for lasting COMMITMENT — you can nurture your relationship along. During a NEW MOON in the Venus-ruled signs of Taurus or Libra, plant an assortment of **flowers** that will surround you with the beauty and energy of sweet DEVOTION.

A few of my proven favorites are listed in the Garden of Indra that follows.

BEFORE YOU PLACE YOUR HOTHOUSE posies or seeds into pots or flowerbeds, bless the ground with a PRAYER OF HEALTH for your plants, yourself, and your relationships.

LIGHT A BLACK CANDLE TO ABSORB and dispel bad energy, and place it in the middle of a circle you have drawn with a stick. Dip your hand into a clay bowl of water and sprinkle drops behind you and before you. Sing out:

Great Spirit, I offer you this petition.
Please cleanse this land—you are the greatest magician.
With my hands, I will plant and sow.
Here, a healing garden will now grow.
Blessings to you and to the Guardians of the Earth.

THE GARDEN *of* INDRA

IN ALL CULTURES, **PARADISE** is a
flower-filled extravaganza. EDEN was a
virtual jungle; Kama Sutra lovers Radha and Krishna
made LOVE among petals, clinging vines,
and scented trees.

PLANTS AND FLOWERS WILL INFUSE
your environment with bliss. Cut flowers in the
bedroom and parlor never fail to CAPTIVATE. As a
horticultural **c o u r t e s a n ,** your lover will come to
appreciate more than just your green thumb!
Try cultivating a few of love's most
captivating blooms:

WALLFLOWER
Cheiranthus cheiri, "Flower of Fidelity"

HAWTHORN
Crataegus oxyacantha, "Flower of the Heart"

YERBA SANTA
Eriodyction glutinosum, "Flower of Emotional Release"

CRANESBILL
Geranium maculatum, "Flower of Constancy"

HONEYSUCKLE
Lonicera caprifolium, "Flower of Unity"

EVENING PRIMROSE
Oenothera biennis, "Flower of Silent Love"

ROSE

Rosa, "Flower of Love"

CLARY SAGE

Salvia sclarea, "Flower of Elation"

LINDEN

Tilia europaea, "Flower of Grace"

PERIWINKLE

Vinca, "Flower of Closeness"

GINGER

Zingiber officinale, "Flower of Paradise"

SENSUAL
Magic

THE ALCHEMICAL MARRIAGE:
SYMBOLIZES THE UNION OF THE OPPOSITES OR THE
UNION OF THE HUMAN AND THE DIVINE.

VENUS ENCHANTMENT

FOR A PASSIONATE PICK-ME-UP,
drink this TASTY TEA with your LOVER.

IN A PINT OF DISTILLED OR SPRING WATER, heat
the root of **ginseng** no less than an hour. Simmer,
don't boil, under cover and don't DARE stir. Pour
yourself a cup for LOVE'S sure power.

BEFORE YOU DRINK this lustful
libation, SIMPLY SAY:

Gift of the Goddess and magic of moon,
May the flower of our love come to full bloom.

SHARED BETWEEN TWO LOVERS before a tryst,
this enchanted potion will give great ENDURANCE
for a memorable encounter.

CONJURING PLEASURE

AT THE NEXT FULL MOON, make a vow,
alone or with your partner, to bring forth all your
EROTIC powers. Begin with a **blissful** bath
in oil-scented water; this essential oil must be the one
that makes you feel SEXIEST. For me, it is an
equal mix of vanilla and amber, which I call
"VAMBER;" it has never failed me. When I
wear this unguent, I feel as if a cloud of
SENSUALITY surrounds me.

SIT IN A DARKENED ROOM, encircled
by flickering jasmine, musk, or "vamber" candles.
RAISE a cup of jasmine tea or a glass of wine from a
vintage that represents a LUCKY year for you, and
speak this spell aloud:

Now I awaken the Goddess in me.
I surrender to love's power.
Tonight I will heat the night with my fire.
As I drink this cup, my juices flower.
I am alive! I am Love! And so it is.

You will **radiate passion** and be
intensely drawn to your lover.

LOVER'S OIL RUB

I ALWAYS GIGGLE when I see over-the-
counter sesame BODY OIL in the pharmacy.
Unknowingly, a woman will apply the oil and never
understand why she feels so much SEXIER and attracts
more glances her way. While that marketplace version
will do in a pinch, a potion you've MADE YOURSELF
will be ten times as EFFECTIVE. You can use
it as a skin softener or as MASSAGE oil.

IN A CUP OF ALMOND OR SESAME OIL, add 20
drops of musk, SANDALWOOD, or orange-blossom oil.
Shake well and HEAT very slowly and carefully. I use a
clay oil warmer with a votive candle beneath,
but the stovetop will do.

WHILE YOU ARE tending the
concoction, look into the candle or gas
flame and whisper:

My lover's eyes are like the sun,
His body like the land,
His skin is soft as rain.
Tonight we are one.

WHEN THE OIL IS A PERFECT TEMPERATURE
to your touch, pour it into a pink bowl and place it
beside the bed. Tenderly undress your lover and
gently lay him down on clean sheets or towels.
With each caress, you will deepen his desire for you
and raise his temperature. Tonight, two lovers
will slide into ECSTASY.

ECSTASY POTION

A TEA OF MANDRAKE root, when **mixed** with
the SWEAT OF A LOVER, can be sprinkled around the
bedroom to heighten ecstasy if accompanied
by this chant:

Brew of mandrake, brew of desire,
Enchant this bed with passion's fire.
Cast a spell of ecstasy.
This is my will. So mote it be.

TANTRIC TRYSTING

TANTRA, A GREATLY OVERUSED and
gravely MISUNDERSTOOD term, comes from the
Sanskrit, meaning "RITUAL, MEDITATION, DISCIPLINE." It
involves a form of mutual worship of the Godhead
(**lingam**) and the Goddesshead (**yoni**), in which
divinity is achieved through the simultaneous EROTIC
and emotional union. This exquisite approach to
deepening the LOVE between you and your partner
requires you to share mutually held intentions.

AT THE NEAREST greenhouse or floral show,
buy as many gardenias as your purse will allow - TEN
OR TWENTY of these heavenly flowers will fill your
bower with a sweet, **seductive** air. Place some of
the flowers in crystal-clear bowls of water, some in a

warm footbath, and SCATTER SOME
PETALS in your bed. Undress and light a single
gardenia-scented candle at the head of the bed.
CRUSH some of the petals and rub them into your
skin and hair, then chant this love spell:

From the soles of your feet to the holy lingam
to the hair that crowns you, I will worship you tonight.
Lover and God – on this evening, I share my entire
being in ecstasy. So mote it be.

WEARING NOTHING but one of the **priceless
blossoms** behind your left ear, greet your lover at
the door. Sit him in the bower bed and worshipfully
wash, dry, and anoint his feet. The lovemaking that
follows will reach new heights of sustained
passion and SPIRITUAL INTENSITY.

APHRODITE'S OIL

FOR MEN, THIS OIL STIMULATES DESIRE
and PROWESS. In a favorite bottle or jar, ideally red
or pink, mix together the following recipe
with a silver spoon:

Five drops rosemary oil
Five drops patchouli
Ten drops yohimbe extract*
A pinch powdered ginseng root
Two tablespoons sesame oil

* available at most herbalists and metaphysical stores

USE THE OIL on your **fingers** to
anoint candles or to **massage** your LOVER'S BODY.
For a chant or spell, you should speak lovingly to the
object of your affections while you rub the MAGIC
massage oil into his skin.

FOR WOMEN: Follow the same instructions
but substitute for the ginseng and yohimbe, which are
greatly stimulating to men, pinches of *saffron* and
ground *dong quai* (also known as angelica root), long
honored in the ORIENT as a
tonic for females.

BELTANE RENDEZVOUS

THIS IS THE *WITCH'S* HIGH HOLIDAY
OF LOVE, observed on APRIL 30th with **feasting**
and CEREMONIAL RITUAL. The Celts of old made
this a day of **wild abandon**, a sexual spree — the
one day of the year when it is okay to make love
outside your relationship. After an all-night PAGAN
love-fest, MAY DAY is celebrated with a ribboned
May Pole and dancing. You decide how you want
your Beltane to go, just as long as it is a fully
sensual experience with food, dance,
sex, and lots of LAUGHTER.

IDEALLY, YOU WILL CELEBRATE BELTANE
outdoors. But if you are indoor-bound, at least
serve the food and drink on the FLOOR, and insist
on **bare feet** and comfy clothes. Serve an ambrosial
spread of finger foods with honeyed mead (available
from some microbreweries), beer, and wine. As you
light INCENSE, set out a few dozen white, red, and
green candles and arrange spring's new flowers —
daffodils and narcissus. With arm extended,
point to each of the four directions and say,
"To the east, to the north," etc.
Then recite:

Hoof and horn, hoof and horn, tonight our spirits are reborn.
Welcome, joy, to my home - fill my friends with love and
laughter. So mote it be.

WHEN YOUR GUESTS ARRIVE, **invite**
them each to LIGHT A CANDLE of their choice and
carve their secret Beltane wish into the wax. Ask them
now to make an **offering** to the ALTAR, which your
invitation instructed them to bring — pink crystals,
an apple for love, or perhaps stone-smooth sea glass
from a beach walk. Sit everyone down to eat, drink,
and make merry. Later, hand out colored ribbons
and flowers to BRAID into other people's hair, or
around wrists, fingers, and toes. It will start getting
markedly more PAGAN now. Turn the volume up
on the music, though live guitars and drums
are better. If your group is open-minded or
of like mind, call a circle and invoke
the randy May spirits.

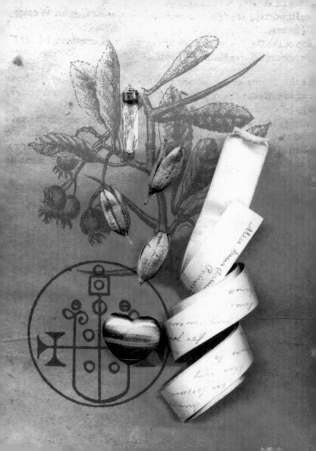

MENDING
Hearts

Sol and Luna

THE SUN NEEDS THE MOON LIKE THE COCK NEEDS THE HEN.
THE SUN AND THE MOON HAVE BOTH HATCHED FROM THE SAME EGG
AND REPRESENT THE ETERNAL ATTRACTION OF OPPOSITES.

THE WISDOM *of the* WIND

HELPING A JILTED FRIEND get over a
BAD RELATIONSHIP is **good medicine**, which
can be therapeutic for you, as well. For example, a
wonderful male co-worker of mine was "dumped"
unceremoniously by a woman he had been seeing for
two years. He quickly went into a DEEP DEPRESSION,
and my heart went out to him. I felt compelled to
help. I knew my friend walked to work each day,
so I decided to let the cleansing winds work a
LITTLE MAGIC on his behalf.

AT THE NEAREST FLORIST, I bought two long-stemmed
white roses. I took the petals from one and mixed
them with a cup of AROMATIC lavender.
I blessed the concoction, chanting:

Eastern wind, wise and free,
Help (name) to see,
A better love will come from thee.

A FEW MINUTES PRIOR to his arrival, I scattered the petals in the wind along his path to work, so he would step on the flowers and release their curative powers. When he arrived at the office that morning, he found the other single LONG-STEMMED ROSE on his desk with a friendly note and invitation to lunch.

His **spirits** improved that very day, and I was blessed with wonderful company.

CALMING OIL

TO HELP HEAL YOURSELF or a BROKENHEARTED **friend**, add five drops of each of the following essential oils to a scentless base oil or almond oil:

wisteria • clove • jojoba • neroli

SHAKE AND ADD a few small rose-quartz crystals into the vial. Offer to give your **heartbroken** friend a neck and head rub. Dab the oil on his or her temples, neck, and shoulders, and gently rub in circular motions. Silently call upon Venus to assist. Offer the CALMING OIL as a gift to your friend to use anytime he or she wants to feel more tranquil.

Charm *for* Clearing Hurt

Friday's Venusian New Moon is the *perfect time* to create a new opportunity and clear away relationship "baggage." Place a bowl of water on your altar. Light two rose-scented pink candles, and a gardenia or vanilla-scented white candle. Burn amber incense in between the candles. Sprinkle salt on your altar cloth and ring a bell, then recite aloud:

Hurt and pain are banished this night;
Fill this heart and home with light!

Ring the bell again. Toss the bowl of water out your front door, and **love troubles** should drain away.

SPELL *for* LETTING GO

AT ONE TIME OR ANOTHER, most
of us have had PROBLEMS giving up on a
RELATIONSHIP. To nip it in the bud, tie a
BLACK STRING around your waist during the
waning moon, when things can be put to rest.
Tie something **symbolic** from the old
relationship to the end of the string —
a photo, a memento, a lock of hair.
Bless a pair of scissors
by chanting:

Bygones be and lovers part,
I'm asking you to leave my heart.
Go in peace, harm to none.
My new life is now begun.

CUT OFF THE STRING and toss away
the **memento** where it will no longer inhabit
your living space. You should feel freer and lighter
IMMEDIATELY and will attract many new
potential paramours now that you are not
weighed down by LOST LOVE.

SPELL *for*
NEW BEGINNINGS

THIS SPELL can be used to MEET
someone NEW or to bring on a NEW PHASE in
an existing relationship. On a MONDAY morning
before dawn, light one pink and one blue candle.
Touch each candle with lily, freesia, or jasmine oil.
Lay a lily on your altar with some catnip. Place a
lapis lazuli stone in front of the lily,
and a glass of water atop
a mirror. Chant:

Healing starts with new beginnings.
My heart is open, I'm ready now.
Today, a new Love I will meet.
Goddess, you will show me how.
So mote it be.

Drink a cup of hot,
honeyed **cinnamon tea** that you stirred
COUNTERCLOCKWISE with a cinnamon stick.
Sprinkle the powdered version of this CHARISMATIC
SPICE on the threshold of your front door and along
your entry path. When the cinnamon powder
is crushed underfoot, its REGENERATIVE
POWERS will help you start a fresh
chapter in your LOVE LIFE.

A Witch's Calendar

January 6
FEAST OF SIRONA, the blessing of the waters.

January 11
CARMENTALIA, a woman's festival
celebrating midwifery and birth.

February 2
CANDLEMAS, when new witches are
initiated with the waxing of winter light.

February 14
APHRODITE'S WEEK,
a festival of love (now Valentine's Day).

March 20
VERNAL EQUINOX, when the mythological
maiden returns above ground with spring.

MARCH 30
FEAST OF FERTILITY, a rite of spring
for planting and sowing.

APRIL 28
FESTIVAL OF FLORA, rituals of
abundance for new flowers and vegetables.

MAY 1
BELTANE, pagan feasting and mating ceremonies
to mark the approach of summer.

JUNE 1
FESTIVAL OF EPIPI, an exploration of the
Full Moon and her mysteries.

JUNE 7
VESTALIA, THE FEAST OF VESTA, the Greek Goddess
of home and hearth.

June 21
SUMMER SOLSTICE, when fire circles honor
Midsummer — the longest day.

July 7
NONAE CAPROTINAE, an ancient Roman custom
celebrating women, with feasts under the fig tree.

July 17
ISIS DAY, when the Egyptian Goddess queen is
honored and embodied.

August 2
LAMMAS DAY, a ritual of remembrance for Earth
Mother and Fortuna.

August 13
FESTIVAL FOR DIANA, the huntress Moon Goddess,
who is worshiped with fires and pilgrimages.

AUGUST 21

CONSUALIA, greeting the coming harvest
with dances, feasting, song, and contests of
speed and strength.

SEPTEMBER 23

AUTUMNAL EQUINOX, the pagan time
for giving thanks.

OCTOBER 31

HALLOWMAS, the Witch's New Year, when the
veil between worlds is thinnest.

DECEMBER 19

OPALIA observes Ops, the ancient Goddess of
farmers and fertility.

DECEMBER 21

WINTER SOLSTICE, the shortest day of the year,
death and rebirth of the Sun.

The
WITCH'S
PANTRY

PENTACLE TO GAIN LOVE:
FORCES THE SPIRITS OF VENUS TO OBEY AND COMPEL.

WHILE YOHIMBE ROOT MIGHT SOUND EXOTIC, every metaphysical five-and-dime has plenty in stock. But just in case, here is a list of resources for you to turn to for herbs, oils, and other tools of magic:

Aphrodisia
264 Bleecker Street
New York, NY 10014
(212) 989-6440

Retail store and mail order for over 200 essential and fragrance oils, as well as herbs, spices, and candles.

Jeanne Rose Aromatherapy Education
and Aromatic Plant Project
219 Carl Street
San Francisco, CA 94117
(415) 564-6785

Mail-order catalog for pure oils, hydrosols, classes, and instruction books.

A.B.L., Exclusive Distributors of Aroma Vera
5901 Rodeo Road
Los Angeles, CA 90016
(800) 669-9514
www.aromavera.com

Stores and catalogs with an extensive selection of essential oils, lamps, and bath salts.

Caprilands Herb Farm
534 Silver Street
Coventry, CT 06238
(860) 742-7244
www.caprilands.com

Retail farm and mail-order resource for seeds, herbal plants, dried herbs, and essential oils.

Frontier Natural Products Co-op
P.O. Box 299
Norway, IA 52318
(800) 669-3275
www.frontiercoop.com

Mail-order resource for herbs, fragrances, spices, and essential oils.

Natural Apothecary of Vermont

334 Grassy Brook Road

Brookline, VT 05345

(802) 365-7156

www.organicoils.com

Mail-order certified organic essential oils.

Real Goods

200 Clara Avenue

Ukiah, CA 95482

(800) 762-7325

www.realgoods.com

Mail-order and retail supplier of candles
and oil lamps.

ILLUSTRATIONS

The illustrations in this book were sourced from the
following publications. Every effort has been made to locate
the holders of copyright of all illustrations, and all were
reprinted in good faith. No attempt has been made to
infringe upon any copyright.

BRENDA KNIGHT

Witch Bree, a.k.a. Brenda Knight,
has been using witchcraft since she was a child.
A poet and medieval scholar, she is a practicing
witch and astrologer. She is a member of the
Reclaiming Institute, a national witchcraft association
founded by the witch Starhawk, as well as the Women's
Spirituality Forum. She leads retreats and
wicca workshops throughout the United States.
Brenda is the author of *Women of the Beat
Generation* (Conari), which won the
American Book Award in 1997.
She lives in San Francisco.

MARGO CHASE

Margo Chase's graphic design prompted
ID magazine to name her one of the top 40
prominent creative people in America today.
She has designed logos for numerous movies,
TV series, and musicians. She created
the design and original collage
illustrations for this book.